Apple Music

Learning to write and play music.

Glee Cathcart

ENRICH/OHAUS
San Jose, California 95131

Graphic Design by Kaye Graphics
Cover and Poster Design by Kaye Quinn
Illustrations by Corb Hillam
Layout Design by Pat Moser

Editorial Direction by Contemporary Ideas, Inc.
Edited by Jim Haugaard
Music Consultant Dona Gustason Louzader

Typography by KGN Graphics

Published by
ENRICH/OHAUS
2325 Paragon Drive
San Jose, CA 95131
U.S.A.

For information on rights and distribution outside the U.S.A., please write ENRICH/OHAUS at the above address.

ISBN: 0-86582-167-4
Catalog No. EN79253
Printed in the United States of America
10 9 8 7 6 5 4 3 2 1

Table of Contents

APPLE MUSIC EN79253 © 1984 ENRICH DIV./OHAUS, San Jose, CA 95131

APPLE MUSIC EN79253 © 1984 ENRICH DIV./OHAUS, San Jose, CA 95131

Introduction

MUSIC AND THE APPLE

The Apple II computers can play music. This book will teach you to program your Apple II Plus or Apple IIe to play some tunes.

You will learn to:

Read simple music from a musical score.

Translate the notes you see into computer music.

Save your music to play later or to include in other programs.

This book will take you, step by step, through the learning process. When you have finished the activities found here, you will have a library of tunes which you can play on your computer.

The book also has these features to help you: a list of programming hints, a chart of notes and their computer values, extra songs for you to program, a glossary of music terms, and the solutions to the activities.

To use the book, you need only type, modify, and run programs which are written for you. You do not need to know the BASIC language. You will be able to play your first song within one hour of the time you sit down at your computer and open this book.

The activities in this book assume that you know the Apple System Commands. If you are not sure how to use RUN, SAVE, LOAD and LIST, study the inside of the front cover. The System Commands are summarized there.

The Apple has some limits as a musical instrument. The lowest possible note is the G below middle C and high notes are very "squeaky". The highest note used in this book is A sharp below high C. The lengths of notes are also limited. A quarter note is given the length 100, a half note 200. Unfortunately, the length for a whole note cannot be set at 400. The largest number possible in Apple Music is 255.

The notes chart inside the back cover is one you will need to use often. You may want to make a copy of this chart and keep it next to your computer.

WHOLE = 250

½ = 125

¼ = 62

⅛ = 31

1/16 = 15

Music Terms and Symbols

𝆹 Whole note   ▬ Whole rest

𝅗𝅥 Half note   ▬ Half rest

𝅘𝅥 Quarter note   𝄽 Quarter rest

𝅘𝅥𝅮 Eighth note   𝄾 Eighth rest

𝅘𝅥𝅯 Sixteenth note   𝄿 Sixteenth rest

A *staff* is a group of five lines on which to place notes.

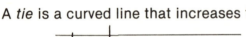

The *treble clef* sign shows that these lines and spaces hold the notes from E above middle C to F.

A *key signature* tells which notes should be sharps or flats.

A *tie* is a curved line that increases the length of the first note by the length of the second note.

A *single bar* marks the end of a measure.

A *double bar* marks the end of a song.

A *sharp* shows that the note should be raised a half-step.

A *flat* shows that the pitch should be a half-step lower.

APPLE MUSIC EN79253 © 1984 ENRICH DIV./OHAUS, San Jose, CA 95131

Tuning Your Computer

Before you begin to play music on an instrument, you must first prepare the instrument by unpacking it, putting it together, or tuning it.

Before you begin to play music on your computer, you must also prepare your "instrument", the computer. You do this by entering and running a special program on your Apple.

This program must be typed *very* carefully. Every number in this program is a command to the computer. If the commands are wrong, the program will not work or will do strange things.

1. Boot an initialized disk.

   (See your DOS manual about initializing a blank disk.)

2. Type NEW and press RETURN.

3. Type this program. Press the RETURN key at the end of each line.

```
100 REM - POKE MUSIC
110 FOR L = 770 TO 790
120 READ V
130 POKE L,V
140 PRINT V
150 GET A$
160 NEXT L
170 DATA 173,48,192,136
180 DATA 208,5,206,1
190 DATA 3,240,9,202
200 DATA 208,245,174,0
210 DATA 3,76,2,3,96
999 END
```

4. Type RUN and press the RETURN key.

   You will see a number on the screen. It should be 173.

5. Press RETURN to go on. The next number should be 48.

   Continue in this way. Compare the numbers you see with the DATA numbers in lines 170 to 210. They must match *exactly*.

   If any of the numbers is incorrect, you will need to retype the whole line which includes that number.

6. Run and correct the program until there are no mistakes.

Look Out!

Running the POKE MUSIC program with incorrect DATA numbers may cause your computer to "freeze". This is *not* a serious problem. If this happens to you, press CTRL and RESET at the same time. Then LIST your program. Check your numbers again and correct any errors.

Testing

It's time to see if your program works. Run your program and then type these lines. (When you see <R>, press RETURN.)

```
POKE 768, 192 <R>
POKE 769,60 <R>
CALL 770 <R>
```

You should hear a single tone. If you want to hear it again, type CALL 770 <R>.

Saving Your Work

It would be lots of work to type this program in every time you wanted music. Luckily, you can save the program on a disk and use it over and over.

Follow these steps:

1. Type 140 <R> and then type 150 <R>.

   (This removes the PRINT statement and the GET statement. You only needed those lines to check your DATA numbers.)

2. Be sure there is an initialized disk in the drive. Then type SAVE POKE MUSIC <R>.

Important

POKE MUSIC places a special machine language program in the Apple's memory. This machine language program is not removed by the command NEW. It is only lost from memory when you turn off the computer.

At the beginning of each "music lesson" on your Apple you *must* run POKE MUSIC before you try to play your own tunes. You only need to run it once; the special program stays in the computer's memory until you turn off the computer.

If you try to run one of your songs and see something like this:

```
0304      A = 03      X = 9D . . . . . . . . . .
*
```

you forgot to run POKE MUSIC before running your song. Press the CTRL and C keys and RETURN to get back to the] prompt. Run POKE MUSIC before you continue with your song.

Experiment

You can change the pitch of the note and its length.

Try these:

```
POKE 768,192 = MIDDLE C
POKE 769,120
CALL 770

POKE 768,114 = A ABOVE MIDDLE C
POKE 769,120
CALL 770
```

Can you see what POKE location 768 does?

Changing the value poked into ==768 changes the *pitch* (high or low sound) of the note.==

Try these:

```
POKE 768,144
POKE 769,240
CALL 770

POKE 768,144
POKE 769,30
CALL 770

POKE 768,144
POKE 769,120
CALL 770
```

What does POKE location 769 do?

Changing the numbers poked into ==769 changes the *length* of the notes.==

Try some pokes of your own. You may poke any whole number from 1 to 255 into 768 and 769. See inside the back cover for some values to try.

```
POKE 768,____
POKE 769,____
CALL 770
```

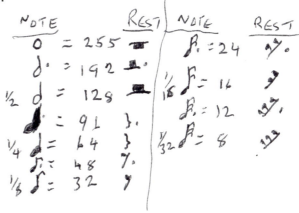

NOTE		REST	NOTE	REST
𝅝	= 255	𝄻	𝅘𝅥. = 24	
𝅗𝅥.	= 192	𝄻.		
½ 𝅗𝅥	= 128	𝄻	⅟₁₆ 𝅘𝅥𝅮 = 16	
𝅘𝅥.	= 91	𝄼.	𝅘𝅥𝅮. = 12	
¼ 𝅘𝅥	= 64	𝄼	⅟₃₂ 𝅘𝅥𝅯 = 8	
𝅘𝅥𝅮.	= 48	𝄽.		
⅛ 𝅘𝅥𝅮	= 32	𝄽		

Scales and Tunes

It was fun to get notes from your Apple. It is more fun if you don't have to type the POKEs and CALLs over and over!

On this page, you will learn to write a *program* which pokes and calls the notes. If you create a tune you like, you can then save the program on your disk and play the tune back again and again.

1. Before you enter any music program, you must prepare the Apple for music by following these steps:

    Boot your music disk.

    Type RUN POKE MUSIC and press RETURN. (You must *always* run POKE MUSIC first. Doing so places the necessary music routine in the Apple's memory.)

    Type NEW and press RETURN.

2. Type this program. Be sure to press RETURN after each line.

```
100  REM - SCALES UP
130  READ P
135  IF P = 0 THEN END
140  POKE 768,P
150  POKE 769,100
160  CALL 770
170  GOTO 130
180  DATA 192,170,150,142,127,114,101,96
980  DATA 0
999  END
```

96 =	C above Middle C
101 =	B
114 =	A
127 =	G
142 =	F
150 =	E
170 =	D
192 =	MIDDLE C

3. Run the program.

    Did you hear a scale of notes going up? If not, LIST your program. Check your typing and retype any incorrect lines. Then run the program again.

4. If your program is correct, save it on your disk.

    Type SAVE SCALES UP and press RETURN.

Experiment

Changes SCALES UP to SCALES DOWN by rearranging the DATA numbers in line 180.

Test and then save SCALES DOWN.

Here are DATA numbers for some other songs.

1. Type RUN POKE MUSIC and press RETURN.

2. Type LOAD SCALES UP and press RETURN.

3. Type the new DATA lines for the song. (The new line 180 will replace line 180 in SCALES UP.)

4. Run the program by typing RUN and pressing RETURN.

5. If you like the song, save it on your disk. Use the name of the song as the name of your program.

FIRST SONG:

```
100 REM - AUNT RHODY

180 DATA 150,150,170,192,192,170,170
190 DATA 142,150,170,192,127,127,142
200 DATA 150,150,150,170,192,170,150,192
```

SECOND SONG:

```
100 REM - BLUE TAIL FLY

180 DATA 134,127,134,150,170,203,203
190 DATA 127,228,170,170,170,181,181
200 DATA 170,150,134
```

If you want to finish Blue Tail Fly, here are the other data lines.

```
210 DATA 127,134,150,150,170,203,203,127
220 DATA 228,228,181,150,127,134,170,170
```

* *

REMEMBER

Whenever you want to run these songs, or any song you have saved on a disk:

1. Type RUN POKE MUSIC and press RETURN.

2. Type RUN *"Your song's name"* and press RETURN.

* *

Lengths of Notes

In order to translate sheet music into computer music, you must learn a special skill called *reading music.*

This section will teach you about the lengths of notes.

Notes can last for different lengths of time:

𝅝 is a whole note

When you add a stem a whole note becomes

𝅗𝅥 a half note.

When you shade in the center, a half note becomes

♩ a quarter note.

When you add one flag, a quarter note becomes

♪ an eighth note.

When you add one more flag, an eighth note becomes

♬ a sixteenth note.

In Apple music, each kind of note has a number to go with it. This number tells the computer how long to sound the note.

KIND	LENGTH	ABBREVIATION
𝅝 Whole	255 *	W
𝅗𝅥 Half	200	H
♩ Quarter	100	Q
♪ Eighth	50	E
♬ Sixteenth	25	S

* The value *should be* 400, but 255 is the largest number which can be used in Apple music.

TRY THIS:

Under each note, write the letter that stands for the kind of note.

Then write the number that tells the note's length.

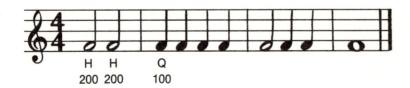

H   H   Q
200 200   100

APPLE MUSIC EN79253 © 1984 ENRICH DIV./OHAUS, San Jose, CA 95131

Now try this one on your own. Write the correct number under each note.

Q
100

Now you will use these number to write a rhythm.

1. Get ready!

> Boot your music disk.
> Type RUN POKE MUSIC and press RETURN.
> Type NEW and press RETURN.

2. Type this program. Be sure to press RETURN at the end of each line.

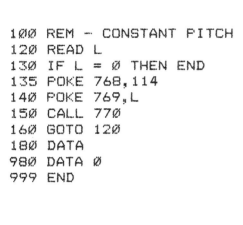

```
100   REM - CONSTANT PITCH
120   READ L
130   IF L = 0 THEN END
135   POKE 768,114
140   POKE 769,L
150   CALL 770
160   GOTO 120
180   DATA
980   DATA 0
999   END
```

Do not run this program. It is not finished yet.

3. You will not usually save an unfinished program, but go ahead and save this one.

> Type SAVE CONSTANT PITCH and press RETURN.

This program is a "skeleton" program. You can change it by adding DATA lines without having to retype the whole program!

4. To finish the program, type this line:

> 180 DATA 100,50,50,100,50,50,200,100,100,255

The numbers in this DATA line should be the same ones you wrote at the top of the page. (If not, check your numbers carefully and see where you made your mistake.)

5. Now, type RUN and press RETURN.

You will hear notes of different lengths.

Rhythms

This activity will give you more practice learning the lengths of notes and using those lengths in programs.

These are the steps to follow:

1. Look at each note. Write the length of the note under the staff.
   (Use W for Whole, H for Half, Q for Quarter, E for Eighth, and S for Sixteenth.)

2. Use the chart at the bottom of this page to find the numbers for the lengths of notes.
   Write the numbers below the letters.

3. Run POKE MUSIC.

4. Type LOAD CONSTANT PITCH and press RETURN.

5. Type LIST and press RETURN.

6. Change DATA line 180 to hold the numbers you wrote in step 2.

7. Run your program. If you like it, save it under a name you have not used before.

Here is a rhythm to try.

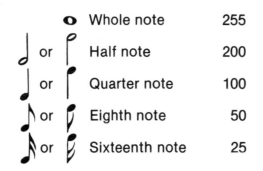

○	Whole note	255
♩ or ⌐	Half note	200
♩ or ⌐	Quarter note	100
♪ or ♪	Eighth note	50
♪ or ♪	Sixteenth note	25

♫ These are two eighth notes joined together, each with a value of 50.

♫ These are two sixteenth notes joined together, each with a value of 25.

More Rhythms

Dotted notes are "in between" notes.

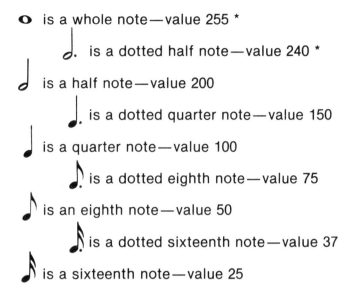

○ is a whole note—value 255 *

♩. is a dotted half note—value 240 *

♩ is a half note—value 200

♩. is a dotted quarter note—value 150

♩ is a quarter note—value 100

♪. is a dotted eighth note—value 75

♪ is an eighth note—value 50

♬ is a dotted sixteenth note—value 37

♬ is a sixteenth note—value 25

Do you see where the dotted notes fit? Putting a dot after a note makes it last one and one-half times as long as the undotted note.

Here are some rhythms which have dotted notes in them. Translate the lengths of the notes into numbers.

Follow the steps on the previous page. Write programs which can play these rhythms. (Write a separate program for each rhythm.)

* The dotted half note should be 300 and the whole note should be 400 to be mathematically accurate. Unfortunately, numbers larger than 255 cannot be used with Apple music, so smaller ones have been used in their place.

Names of Notes

You have learned about the lengths of notes. Now you need to learn about *pitch.* The pitch of a note is its sound, high or low.

Each pitch has a letter name from A to G.

Here are letter names of the *spaces.*

Notice that they spell the word FACE.

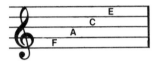

You need to learn the letter names of the spaces.

Here are some puzzles to solve. Just write the names of the notes under the music. Then write them, in order, on the lines in the sentences.

A famous cartoon dog is also a World War I flying ___ ___ ___ .

The dog loves to flirt with girls in a French ___ ___ ___ ___ .

If he's not careful, the waitress will throw his root beer in his ___ ___ ___ ___ .

The *lines* of the musical staff also have letter names.

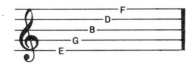

One old trick for learning the names of the lines is to memorize the words *Every Good Boy Does Fine.* The first letter of each word stands for the name of a note that is on a line.

Here is another puzzle. Write the letter names under the notes. Then write them on the lines in the sentences.

A hungry cat will ___ ___ ___ to be ___ ___ ___ and then will go to ___ ___ ___ .

This puzzle uses the names of the lines *and* the spaces.

On a visit to the zoo, I saw a chimp in a ___ ___ ___ ___ . His ___ ___ ___ ___ was sad. He ___ ___ ___ ___ ___ ___ to be ___ ___ ___ . The keeper put the chimp's ___ ___ ___ ___ , six bananas, in a ___ ___ ___ . Then the chimp went to ___ ___ ___ .

Using Pitch

The names of the notes must be changed into numbers for the computer. The numbers tell the computer the correct *pitch* for the note.

Here are the names and numbers:

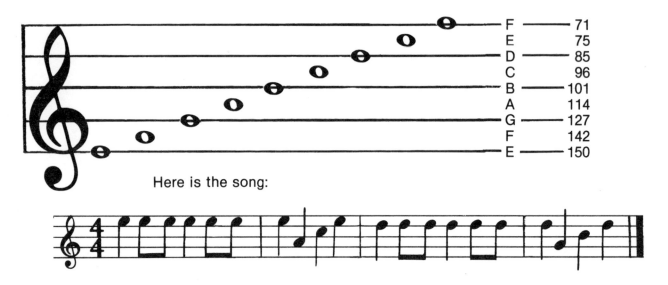

Note	Number
F	71
E	75
D	85
C	96
B	101
A	114
G	127
F	142
E	150

Here is the song:

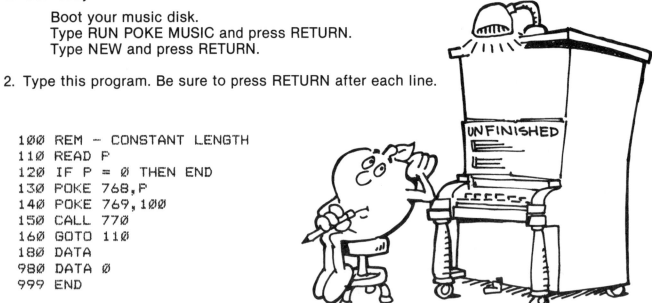

Under each note, write the letter for the pitch of that note. Then write the number that goes with that pitch.

Now write a program using these notes.

1. Get ready.

   Boot your music disk.
   Type RUN POKE MUSIC and press RETURN.
   Type NEW and press RETURN.

2. Type this program. Be sure to press RETURN after each line.

```
100 REM - CONSTANT LENGTH
110 READ P
120 IF P = 0 THEN END
130 POKE 768,P
140 POKE 769,100
150 CALL 770
160 GOTO 110
180 DATA
980 DATA 0
999 END
```

Do not run this program. It is not finished yet.

3. Type SAVE CONSTANT LENGTH and press RETURN.

To finish this program you must add DATA lines.

4. Type 180 DATA (do not press RETURN).

5. Look at the numbers you wrote below the notes.

   Type the first ten of those numbers after the word DATA in line 180.

   Separate the numbers with commas.

   Do *not* place a comma after the last number.

   Press RETURN when the line is finished.

   Type 190 DATA and finish the line using the rest of the notes.

   DATA lines should always be short! Short lines are easy to retype if you make an error.

6. Now, type RUN and press RETURN.

   If your program sounds right, save it on your disk as SAILOR. If not, check the numbers you wrote down under the notes.

   Fix them if they need it. Follow these steps:

   > Check the numbers you wrote under the music against the numbers given for the lines and spaces of the staff.

   > If the numbers on your music are correct, check the numbers in the DATA statements in your program. To do this, type LIST <R> and be sure the numbers following the word DATA are correct.

   Test the program by running it again. Continue to make corrections until the song sounds right.

7. When you are finished with the song, save it as SAILOR.

* *

REMEMBER:

Whenever you want to run this song, or any song you have saved on a disk:

1. Type RUN POKE MUSIC and press RETURN.

2. Type RUN "*Your song's name*" and press RETURN.

* *

APPLE MUSIC EN79253 © 1984 ENRICH DIV./OHAUS, San Jose, CA 95131

Ledger Lines

You have now written music which uses nine different notes.

There are more notes to be used. Some of them are not on the lines or spaces of the staff but are written above or below the staff.

Here are the other notes you will want to learn to write computer music:

Note	Number
A	56
G	63
F	71
E	75
D	85
C	96
B	101
A	114
G	127
F	142
E	150
D	170
C (MIDDLE C)	192
B	203
A	228
G	255

The lines through A and C are called *ledger lines*. You can see more *ledger lines* on the "stems" of B and G.

Because the range of notes possible on the Apple is limited, you will only use the notes listed above in your songs.

No note below the low G is possible. 255 is the largest number that can be poked into any memory location.

Higher notes are possible, but they sound very "squeaky".

Here is another puzzle. This one includes notes above and below the staff.

Write down the names of the notes and then put the letters on the lines in the sentence.

My cat ___ ___ ___ ___ will ___ ___ ___ for a ___ ___ ___ of ___ ___ ___ ___ .

APPLE MUSIC EN79253 © 1984 ENRICH DIV./OHAUS, San Jose, CA 95131

Here is another song for you to program. For now, ignore the different lengths of the notes. (The next section will tell you how to combine pitch changes and length changes in one song.)

After you have written the correct number under each note:

1. Boot your music disk.
   Type RUN POKE MUSIC and press RETURN.
   Type NEW and press RETURN.

2. Type LOAD CONSTANT LENGTH and press RETURN.

3. Change line 180 to use the numbers for the first two measures of this tune.

   (A *measure* of music is the part between two vertical lines.)

   Be sure to begin the line with the word DATA and place commas between the numbers. Press RETURN at the end of the line.

4. Continue to write new DATA lines for the rest of the song.

   Use line numbers from 190 to 900.

   Be sure to keep your DATA lines short!

5. Test and correct your program. When it is right, save it as VOLGA BOATMAN.

Pitch and Length

You have learned about the *length* and *pitch* of notes.

It is time to put pitch and length *together* in one song.

PITCH   150
LENGTH 200

Beneath each note, write *two* numbers, the top one for pitch, and the bottom one for the length of the note.

The numbers have been started for you. Finish labeling the notes. (You may need the chart inside the back cover to help you.)

When the notes are all labeled, follow these steps to program the music:

1. Boot your music disk and run POKE MUSIC.
    Type NEW and press RETURN

2. Enter this program:

```
100  REM - MAKE MUSIC
110  READ P
120  READ L
125  IF P = Ø THEN END
130  POKE 768,P
140  POKE 769,L
150  CALL 770
160  GOTO 110
170  DATA
900  DATA Ø,Ø
999  END
```

3. Save this "skeleton" program under the name MAKE MUSIC.

4. Retype line 170 this way:

   170 DATA 150,200, 170,50 192,50 150,50 170,50

   Notice that the DATA is grouped by twos.

   The first DATA number in each pair is the *pitch.* The second number is the *length.*

   The spaces between the pairs of DATA were made by pressing the space bar twice.

   If you use spaces to group your DATA by twos, it will be much easier to check and correct your notes!

5. The DATA in line 170 is for the notes in the first measure (between the first two vertical lines.)

   Create a DATA line 180 that holds the numbers for the next measure (the next four notes).

   Set it up like line 170.

   Continue to write DATA lines until the tune is finished.

   NOTE: You can have all the DATA lines you need! Just do not give one a line number greater than 899. (The zeros in line 900 are "flags" which mark the end of the song.)

   It is a good idea to keep your DATA lines short. Short lines take less time to retype if you make an error!

6. Test the program. If it is not correct, type LIST and press RETURN. Then check your typing. Remember, every number counts!

7. Save your program as SWANEE RIVER.

* *

REMEMBER:

Whenever you want to run this song, or any song you have saved on disk:

1. Type RUN POKE MUSIC and press RETURN.

2. Type RUN "Your song's name" and press RETURN.

* *

Debugging Hints

Every programmer makes mistakes. These mistakes are so common that there is a special word for them. Programming mistakes are called "bugs".

If you are having trouble with your DATA lines, it is time to go "bug hunting".

1. Run POKE MUSIC and then type NEW.

2. Type LOAD MAKE MUSIC and press RETURN.

3. Type LIST and press RETURN.

You should see

```
100 REM - MAKE MUSIC
110 READ P
120 READ L
125 IF P = 0 THEN END
130 POKE 768,P
140 POKE 769,L
150 CALL 770
160 GOTO 110
170 DATA
900 DATA 0,0
999 END
```

4. Type these three lines. Press RETURN after each line.

```
115 LET C = C + 1

122 PRINT C,P,L

155 GET A$
```

Here is how the lines can help you:

Line 115 puts a counter in your program. This will make it possible to know which note is being played. (Number 1, 2, 3, etc.)

Line 122 prints the number of the note (C), the pitch value (P) and the length value (L) on the screen just before the note sounds.

Line 155 makes the computer wait until you press a key to go on.

Let's test the program:

5. Type DATA line 170 this way:

```
170 DATA  142,100,   170,150,   114,50
```

APPLE MUSIC

Length of notes

𝅝	whole note	255
𝅗𝅥.	dotted half	240
𝅗𝅥	half note	200
𝅘𝅥.	dotted quarter	150
𝅘𝅥	quarter note	100
𝅘𝅥𝅮.	dotted eighth	75
𝅘𝅥𝅮	eighth note	50
𝅘𝅥𝅯.	dotted sixteenth	37
𝅘𝅥𝅯	sixteenth note	25

Names of notes and their values

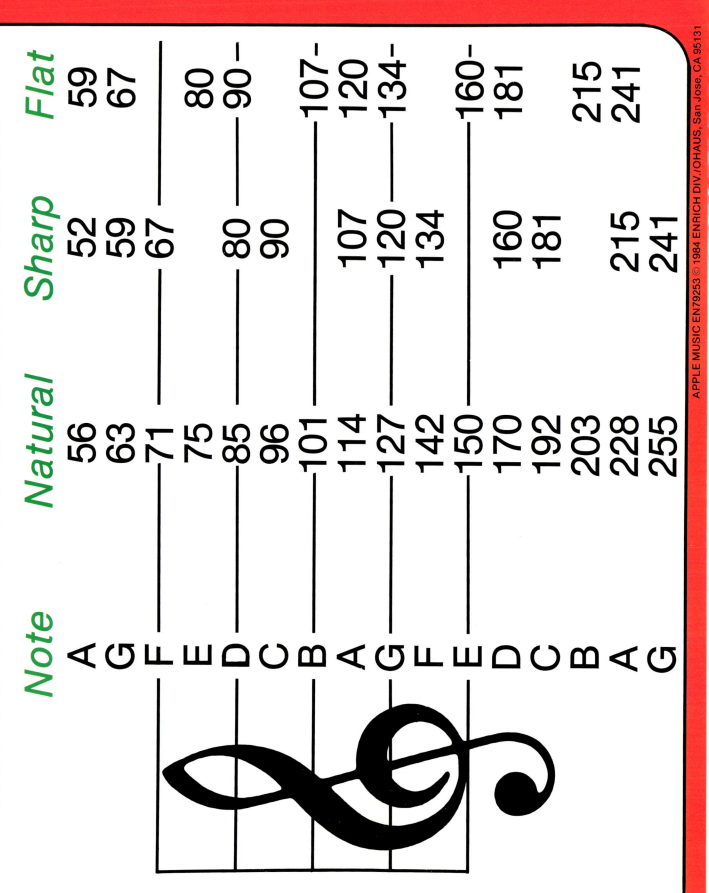

Note	Natural	Sharp	Flat
A	56	52	59
G	63	59	67
F	71	67	
E	75		80
D	85	80	90
C	96	90	
B	101		107
A	114	107	120
G	127	120	134
F	142	134	
E	150		160
D	170	160	181
C	192	181	
B	203		215
A	228	215	241
G	255	241	

APPLE MUSIC EN 79253 © 1984 ENRICH DIV./OHAUS, San Jose, CA 95131

6. Run the program. (Just type RUN, not RUN MAKE MUSIC.)

You will see this on the screen:

           1   142   100

Then you will hear a note.

Press any key to go on and the program will continue.

           2   170   150

           3   114   50

Here is a tune and a DATA line to go with it. The DATA is *not* correct. Type the DATA line as it is even if you know where the error is.

```
170 DATA 192,200,  192,50,  192,100,  170,100,  150,200
180 DATA 192,100,  170,100,  150,100,  142,100,  127,255
```

Type RUN and press RETURN. Listen for a "sour" note or one of the wrong length. When you hear the error, write down the three numbers just printed.

Now, look at the music. Count the notes until you find the one which was given the wrong number. Give it the correct number.

Next, look at the DATA line. Count the pairs of numbers until you find the pair which has an error.

Now retype the whole DATA line correctly. Then RUN <R>.

These debugging tools are very helpful, but you would not want them in your final music program. After your program is correct, remove lines 115, 122, and 155. Do this by typing 115 <R> 122 <R> and 155 <R>.

Here is the rest of the song. Do you recognize the tune?

Song Writing

You now know how to program music with varying pitch and length of notes.

This is a good time to improve some of the music you have already programmed.

1. Run POKE MUSIC. Then load SAILOR.

2. Type LIST and press RETURN. Write down the DATA numbers in lines 180 to 190.

3. Write the numbers under these notes:

     75 *PITCH*
   100 *LENGTH*

4. The numbers you have written down represent the *pitch* of the notes. Under the pitch numbers, write the numbers for the length of the notes.

5. Load MAKE MUSIC.

```
100  REM - MAKE MUSIC
110  READ P
120  READ L
125  IF P = 0 THEN END
130  POKE 768,P
140  POKE 769,L
150  CALL 770
160  GOTO 110
170  DATA
980  DATA 0,0
999  END
```

6. Type 170 DATA followed by p,l, p,l, p,l where p is the pitch for each note and l is the length.

    Example:

    ```
    170 DATA 75,100,  75,50,  75,50,  75,100
    ```

    Type as many DATA lines as you need to finish the song.

7. Run your program by typing RUN and pressing RETURN. Do NOT type RUN SAILOR! If you do this you will load the *old* version from the disk and erase the new one!

8. Correct any errors. SAVE SAILOR <R>.

Follow the same steps to improve VOLGA BOATMAN. Here is the music for that song again.

VOLGA BOATMAN

Here is a new song for you to try:

ODE TO JOY

Practice

Here are some songs to practice.

Remember to follow these steps:

1. Write the numbers for pitch and length under each note.
   (Use the chart on the inside of the back cover.)

2. Run POKE MUSIC.

3. Load MAKE MUSIC.

4. Type LIST and press RETURN.

5. Write the DATA lines you need. Use line numbers from 170 to 890.
   Be sure to keep your DATA lines short!

6. Test your song. If necessary, use the debugging techniques from page 24.

7. Save your song.

AMAZING GRACE

A - maz - ing Grace, How sweet the sound, That

saved a wretch like me; I once was lost, but

now am found; Was blind, but now I see.

AURA LEE

WORRIED MAN BLUES

It takes a wor-ried man to sing a wor-ried song, It

takes a wor-ried man to sing a wor-ried song, It

takes a wor-ried man to sing a wor-ried song, I'm wor-ried

now, yes now, but I won't be wor-ried long.

Words and Music

Many songs have words to sing. It is easy to program songs with words!

1. RUN POKE MUSIC. Then load the program MAKE MUSIC.

2. Add these lines:

```
105 READ W$
145 PRINT W$;
```

3. Change this line:

```
900 DATA 0,0,0
```

4. Save this new "skeleton" program as MUSIC WORDS.

Here is a program that "sings" a song:

```
100 REM - MUSIC WORDS
105 READ W$
110 READ P
120 READ L
125 IF P = 0 THEN END
130 POKE 768,P
140 POKE 769,L
145 PRINT W$;
150 CALL 770
160 GOTO 105
170 DATA ROW ,192,200,  ROW ,192,200,  ROW ,192,100
180 DATA YOUR ,170,100,  BOAT ,150,200,  GENT ,150,100
190 DATA LY ,170,100,  DOWN ,150,100,  THE ,142,100
200 DATA STREAM ,127,255
900 DATA 0,0,0
999 END
```

Notice the spaces after the words in the DATA lines. They must be there to keep the words from running together on the screen.

Here is the music if you want to finish the song.

APPLE MUSIC EN79253 © 1984 ENRICH DIV./OHAUS, San Jose, CA 95131

30

When you ran the program on page 30, you saw the words on the screen. In the middle of some of the words, there were unwanted spaces.

If a whole word is to be printed, press the space bar after the word.

```
170 DATA HE'S ,101,200...
```

If a first or middle syllable is to be printed, do *not* press the space bar after the syllable.

```
170 DATA HE'S ,101,200,  A , 101,100,   JOL,101,100
```

When programming this next song, print a space *only* at the end of a word.

He's   a   jol - ly   good   fel - low,   For   he's   a   jol - ly   good

fel - low,   For   he's   a   jol - ly   good   fel - -

low,   Which   no - bod - y   can   de - ny.

Here are the DATA lines for the first four measures:

```
170 DATA HE'S ,101,200,  A ,101,100,   JOL,101,100,  LY ,114,100
180 DATA GOOD ,101,100,  FEL,96,240,   LOW ,101,200,   FOR ,101,100
```

Notice that there is no space after JOL and FEL. Since there is no space in the DATA, LY will be printed directly after JOL to make JOLLY, and LOW will join with FEL to make FELLOW.

Load MUSIC WORDS. Type DATA lines 170 and 180. Then finish the song by adding more data lines.

Practice, Practice

Here are songs with words for you to practice.

Remember to follow these steps:

1. Write the numbers for pitch and length under each note.
    (Use the chart on the inside of the back cover.)

2. Run POKE MUSIC.

3. Load MUSIC WORDS.

4. Type LIST and press RETURN.

5. Write the DATA lines you need. Use line numbers from 170 to 890.
    Your DATA lines should have this form:
    170 DATA WORD1 , pitch 1,length 1, WORD2 ,pitch 2,length 2
    (The DATA must be in groups of *three!*)
    Be sure you keep your DATA lines short!

6. Test your song. If necessary, use the debugging techniques from page 24.

7. Save your song.

SKIP TO MY LOU

Lost   my   part - ner,   what'll I   do?   Lost my part - ner ,   what'll I   do?

Lost my part - ner,   what'll I   do?   Skip to my Lou my   dar - ling.

APPLE MUSIC EN79253 © 1984 ENRICH DIV./OHAUS, San Jose, CA 95131

FRERES JACQUES

Fre-re Jac-ques, fre-re Jac-ques, Dor-mez vous? Dor-mez vous?
Are you sleep-ing? Are you sleep-ing? Broth-er John, broth-er John,

Son-nez les ma-tin - es, son-nez les ma-tin - es, din, din, don; din, din don.
Morn-ing bells are ring - ing, morn-ing bells are ring - ing, ding, dong, ding; ding, dong, ding.

This next song includes some rests (🜛). Ignore these for now. You will learn to use rests on pages 40 to 42.

TOM DOOLEY

Hang down your head, Tom Doo-ley, Hang down your head and cry.

Hang down your head, Tom Doo-ley, Poor boy you're bound to die.

Met her on the moun-tain and there I took her life. Met her

on the moun -tain stabbed her with my knife.

Sharps and Flats

Here is a picture of part of a piano keyboard.

Notice there are both white and black keys.

Black keys give half steps.

The black key between F and G gives a note which is half way between F and G.

That note is called F sharp (F#) or G flat (G ♭).

Sharps and flats are used when you have a song which needs half tones.

1. Run POKE MUSIC. Then load SCALES UP.

2. List the program. Line 180 should look like this:

        180 DATA 192,170,150,142,127,114,101,96

    The notes are:

        C   D   E   F   G   A   B   .C

3. Type RUN and press RETURN to hear the scale.

This scale is in the key of C because it begins with a C.

The key signature at the left end of the staff will look like this:

There are no sharps (#)
and no flats (♭).

4. Change line 180 to look like this:

        180 DATA 255,228,203,192,170,150,142,127

    The notes are:

        G   A   B   C   D   E   F   G

5. Run the program. The seventh note should sound too low. This note, F, must be moved from a white key to the next black key, F sharp (F#).

6. Change line 180 again:

        180 DATA 255,228,203,192,170,150,134,127

   The notes are:

        G   A   B   C   D   E   F# G

7. Type RUN and press RETURN. It should sound better this time!

   This is called the key of G because it begins with G.

   The key signature should look like this:

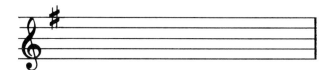

   There is one sharp.
   The F is sharped.

Sometimes the pitch of a note will need to be lower. When a note is lowered by one-half step, the black note is called a flat (♭).

8. Type this DATA line and test it by running the program:

        180 DATA 142,127,114,101,96,84,75,71

   The notes are:

        F   G   A   B   C   D   E   F

   The fourth note, B, sounds too high. It should be lowered one-half tone to the black key below B. This key is called B flat (B♭).

9. Type this new DATA line and run the program:

        180 DATA 142,127,114,107,96,84,75,71

   The notes are:

        F   G   A   B♭ C   D   E   F

   This scale is in the key of F.

   The key signature should look like this:

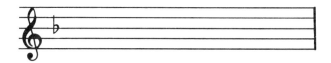

   There is one flat.
   It is B flat (B♭).

Songs can have more than one sharp or flat. The next four pages will help you learn which notes to make into sharps or flats.

Using Sharps

Sharps are "half-way" notes. For example, a C sharp is halfway between a C and a D.

The number values of sharps are halfway between the note named and the next note up the scale.

The value of middle C is 192. The value of the next note, D, is 170. The value of C sharp is 181 (halfway between 170 and 192).

Here is a chart you will need:

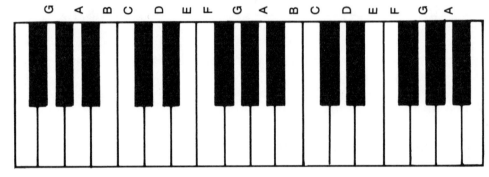

Here is the key signature of a song:

On which line is the sharp?

This means that *all* F's in this song must be sharped.

Every note in these places must be sharp.

Here is another key signature:

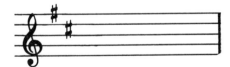

What notes must be sharps?

All F's and C's must be F#'s and C#'s.

Every note in these places must be a sharp.

Here is a song for you to program. (This song has some special symbols, called "rests". Ignore the rests for now. Pages 40 through 42 will teach you how to use rests.)

SHENANDOAH

1. What line is the sharp on? Remember that *every* note with that name in this song *must* be a sharp!

   Go through the song and circle each note that must be a sharp.

   (Hint: there should be 2 of them)

2. Under each note in the song, write its pitch and its length.

3. Run POKE MUSIC then load MAKE MUSIC.

4. Add DATA lines to the program. Use line numbers between 170 and 899. Use the numbers you wrote under the notes as the DATA numbers.

5. Run the program. If it sounds correct, save it. If not, change the DATA lines until the song is correct. (Don't forget the debugging methods on page 24.)

If a song has more than one sharp, the steps for programming are the same as the steps shown above.

Using Flats

Flats are also "half-way" notes. The pitch of a flat is lower than that of a "natural" note. G flat is one half step below G. A G flat is halfway between F and G.

The number values of flats are halfway between the note named and the next note down the scale.

The value of middle C is 192. The value of the next lower note, D, is 170. The value of D flat is 181 (halfway between 170 and 192).

Here is a chart you will need:

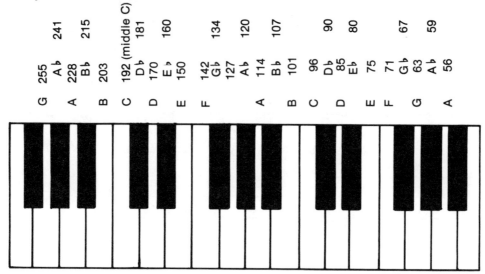

Here is the key signature of a song:

On which line is the flat?

This means that *all* B's in the song must be flatted.

Every note in these places must be a B flat.

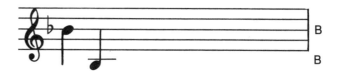

Here is another key signature:

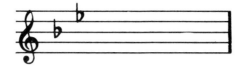

What notes must be flats?

All B's and E's in this song must be B flats and E flats.

Every note in these places must be a flat.

Here is the song for you to program:

Mi - chael   row   the   boat   a -shore,   Hal-le   -lue   -jah!

Mi - chael   row   the   boat   a -shore,   Hal-le   -lu -   jah!

1. What line is the flat on? Remember that *every* note with that name in this song *must* be a flat!
    Go through the song and circle each note that must be a flat.
    (Hint: there should be 1 of them)

2. Under each note in the song, write its pitch and its length.

3. Run POKE MUSIC then load MAKE MUSIC.

4. Add DATA lines to the program. Use line numbers between 170 and 899. Use the numbers you
    wrote under the notes as the DATA numbers.

5. Run the program. If it sounds correct, save it. If not, change the DATA lines until the song is
    correct. (Don't forget the debugging methods on page 24.)

If a song has more than one flat, the steps for programming the song are the same as steps 1-5
above.

Rests

When you listen to a song, you will often hear pauses. These pauses are called *rests.*

Rests come in different lengths:

     ▬   is a whole rest   – pauses the length of a whole note

     ▬   is a half rest   – pauses the length of a half note

     𝄽   is a quarter rest   – pauses the length of a quarter note

     𝄾   is an eighth rest   – pauses the length of an 8th note

     𝄿   is a sixteenth rest– pauses the length of a 16th note

Here are parts of some songs. Go through each one and circle the rests. Then label each rest with a letter (W for Whole, H for Half, Q for Quarter, E for Eighth, or S for Sixteenth.)

Music with Rests

To use rests in Apple music, you will need to use some special programming techniques.

FOR-NEXT loops:

You can make the computer pause by using a FOR-NEXT loop like this:

100 for P = 1 to 200:NEXT P

The computer will pause while it counts from 1 to 200. By changing 200 to another number, you can lengthen or shorten the pause.

GOSUB-RETURN:

When you are writing a program, you may want to use one programming routine over and over. It would be very tiresome to type such a routine again and again.

With GOSUB and RETURN you can create *subroutines.* Subroutines are a part of a program which can be used again and again.

Here is how to use subroutines and pauses to add rests to your music:

1. Load the program MAKE MUSIC. It should look like this:

```
100 REM - MAKE MUSIC
110 READ P
120 READ L
125 IF P = 0 THEN END
130 POKE 768,P
140 POKE 769,L
150 CALL 770
160 GOTO 110
900 DATA 0
999 END
```

2. Change line 100 to: REM-MUSIC RESTS

3. Add these lines:

```
126 IF L = 1 THEN GOSUB 1000:GOTO 160
127 IF L = 2 THEN GOSUB 2000:GOTO 160
128 IF L = 4 THEN GOSUB 3000:GOTO 160
129 IF L = 8 THEN GOSUB 4000:GOTO 160
```

```
1000 REM - WHOLE REST
1010 FOR P = 1 TO 800:NEXT P
1020 RETURN

2000 REM - HALF REST
2010 FOR P = 1 TO 400:NEXT P
2020 RETURN

3000 REM - QUARTER REST
3010 FOR P = 1 TO 200:NEXT P
3020 RETURN

4000 REM - EIGHTH REST
4010 FOR P = 1 TO 100:NEXT P
4020 RETURN
```

4. Save this "skeleton" program as MUSIC RESTS.

5. Add DATA lines to your program. Use line numbers from 170 to 890.

Here is a song and the DATA for its first line:

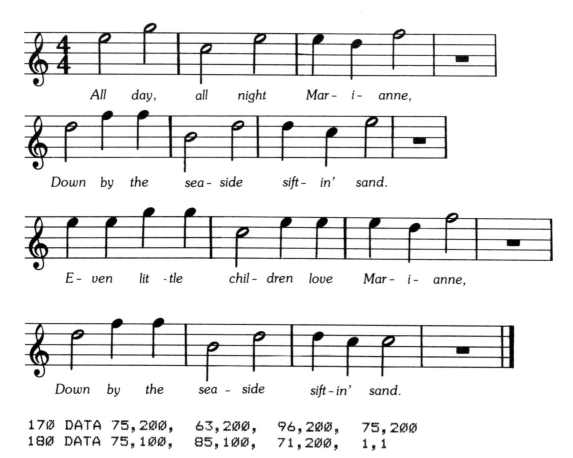

```
170 DATA 75,200,    63,200,    96,200,    75,200
180 DATA 75,100,    85,100,    71,200,    1,1
```

Notice the use of the number 1. The 1 is a "flag" which tells the computer to use the subroutine at 1000.

There must be *two* 1's. Lines 110 and 120 must *both* have values to read.

Finish the song. Be sure to include the rests.

Practice, Practice, Practice

To play an instrument well, you need lots of practice. To program your computer to play music you will also need practice. The pages of this section include some songs for you to try.

For these songs, use one of the skeleton programs.

1. Run POKE MUSIC.

2. Load MAKE MUSIC or MUSIC WORDS or MUSIC RESTS.

3. Add the necessary DATA lines.

4. Run your program. Correct the lines if necessary.

5. Save your program.

These songs have sharps or flats. The programming steps are the same, but you need to be careful when choosing DATA numbers.

The extra steps to writing DATA lines for sharps or flats are:

1. Look at the key signature. Which notes must be sharped or flatted?

2. Go through the music, circle the notes which should be sharps or flats.

3. Write your DATA lines. Be sure you use the correct values for the sharps and flats.

TELL ME WHY

Tell me why the stars do shine,

Tell me why the i - vy twines,

Tell me why the o-cean's blue,

And I will tell you just why I love you.

If you want to use words with MUSIC RESTS, add these lines to your MUSIC RESTS program:

```
105 READ W$
145 PRINT W$;
900 DATA 0,0,0
```

The DATA numbers for rests in a program with words must look like this:

"",1,1   or   "",2,2   or   "",4,4

The "" prints no word on the screen. (Remember, the singer is resting!)

HE'S GOT THE WHOLE WORLD IN HIS HANDS

Programming Hints:

Playing your music:

If you try to run a music program and see something like this:

    0304 A = 03 X = 9D . . . .
    *

You forgot to run POKE MUSIC before running your song.

Press CTRL C and RETURN to return to the] prompt. Then run POKE MUSIC. Then run your song.

Correcting typing errors

If you see your mistake before you press RETURN:

Using the left arrow, back up and correct the error, then use the right arrow to go past the end of the line before you press RETURN.

If you see your mistake after typing RETURN:

Retype the entire line correctly and press RETURN.

If you leave out a line:

Just type it in. The computer will put the lines in order.

Correcting programming errors:

SYNTAX ERRORS in (line number)

List that line by typing LIST (line number) <R>.
Compare the line to the line on the page.
Retype the line correctly.

NOTE: If the SYNTAX ERROR message refers to a DATA line, check your READ lines carefully. Be sure you are using the correct variables (L, P or W$) in the right order.

If this error message happens when you are writing a song with words, check your DATA lines carefully. Your DATA may be out of order. This will make the computer try to read a word when it is looking for a number!

OUT OF DATA ERROR

Check line 900. Be sure it has the correct number of zeros.

FILE NOT FOUND

Catalog your disk to check the spelling of the title of your program. You may have typed the name wrong.

Answers:

Here are the correct DATA lines for the activities.

The line numbers and the length of the DATA lines may vary.

Page 14

180 DATA 200,100,200,100,100,50,50
190 DATA 100,100,200

Page 15

FIRST RHYTHM:
180 DATA 240,100,100,200,100,150,50
190 DATA 100,100,200,200

SECOND RHYTHM:
180 DATA 200,100,100,100,50,50
190 DATA 100,50,50,240,100,100,240

THIRD RHYTHM:
180 DATA 240,200,100,50,50,50,50,50,50,240

Pages 16-17

ACE	CAFE	FACE
BEG	FED	BED
CAGE	FACE	BEGGED
FED	FEED	BAG	BED

Pages 18-19

SAILOR:
180 DATA 75,75,75,75,75,75,75,114,96,75
190 DATA 85,85,85,85,85,85,85,127,101,85

Page 20

GABE   BEG   BAG   BEEF

Page 21

VOLGA BOATMAN:
180 DATA 192,228,170,228,203,192
190 DATA 228,170,228,203,192,142
200 DATA 150,150,170,192,228,170,228

Pages 22-23

SWANEE RIVER:
170 DATA 150,200, 170,50, 192,50, 150,50, 170,50
180 DATA 192,100, 96,100, 114,50, 96,150
190 DATA 127,200, 150,100, 192,100
200 DATA 170,255

Pages 24-25

ROW, ROW, ROW YOUR BOAT:

FIRST FOUR MEASURES:
170 DATA 192,200, 192,200, 192,100, 170,100
180 DATA 150,200, 150,100, 170,100, 150,100
190 DATA 142,100, 127,255

LAST FOUR MEASURES:
200 DATA 96,50, 96,50, 96,100, 127,50, 127,50
210 DATA 127,100, 150,50, 150,50, 150,100
220 DATA 192,50, 192,50, 192,100, 127,100
230 DATA 142,100, 150,100, 170,100, 192,255

Pages 26-27

SAILOR:
170 DATA 75,100, 75,50, 75,50, 75,100
180 DATA 75,50, 75,50, 75,100, 114,100
190 DATA 96,100, 75,100, 85,100, 85,50
200 DATA 85,50, 85,100, 85,50, 85,50
210 DATA 85,100, 127,100, 101,100, 85,100

VOLGA BOATMAN:
170 DATA 192,100, 228,100, 170,200, 228,240
180 DATA 203,100, 192,100, 228,100, 170,200
190 DATA 228,240, 203,100, 192,200, 142,200
200 DATA 150,100, 150,100, 170,200, 192,100
210 DATA 228,100, 170,200, 228,255

Pages 26-27 (cont.)

ODE TO JOY:

```
170 DATA 75,100, 75,100, 71,100, 63,100
180 DATA 63,100, 71,100, 75,100, 85,100
190 DATA 96,100, 96,100, 85,100, 75,100
200 DATA 75,100, 85,100, 85,200, 75,100
210 DATA 75,100, 71,100, 63,100, 63,100
220 DATA 71,100, 75,100, 85,100, 96,100
230 DATA 96,100, 85,100, 75,100, 85,100
240 DATA 96,100, 96,200
```

Pages 28-29

AMAZING GRACE:

```
170 DATA 170,100, 127,200, 101,100, 101,200
180 DATA 114,100, 127,200, 150,100, 170,200
190 DATA 170,100, 127,200, 101,100, 101,200
200 DATA 114,100, 85,200, 101,100, 85,200
210 DATA 101,100, 127,200, 150,100, 127,200
220 DATA 150,100, 170,200, 170,200, 127,200
230 DATA 101,100, 101,200, 114,100, 127,200
```

AURA LEE:

```
170 DATA 127,100, 96,100, 101,100, 96,100
180 DATA 85,100, 114,100, 85,200, 96,100
190 DATA 101,100, 114,100, 101,100, 96,200
200 DATA 127,200, 127,100, 96,100, 101,100
210 DATA 96,100, 85,100, 114,100, 85,200
220 DATA 96,100, 101,100, 114,100, 101,100
230 DATA 96,255, 75,100, 75,100, 75,200
240 DATA 75,100, 75,100, 75,200, 75,100
250 DATA 85,100, 96,100, 85,100, 75,255
260 DATA 75,100, 75,100, 71,100, 75,100
270 DATA 85,100, 114,100, 85,200, 96,100
280 DATA 101,100, 114,100, 101,100, 96,255
```

WORRIED MAN BLUES:

```
170 DATA 170,100, 170,150, 170,50, 170,150
180 DATA 150,50, 127,240, 114,100, 101,150
190 DATA 101,50, 101,150, 114,50, 127,240
200 DATA 127,100, 150,150, 150,50, 150,150
210 DATA 127,50, 127,240, 150,100, 127,150
220 DATA 127,50, 127,150, 150,50, 170,240
230 DATA 170,100, 170,150, 170,50, 170,150
240 DATA 150,50, 127,240, 114,100, 101,150
250 DATA 101,50, 101,150, 114,50, 127,150
260 DATA 127,50, 127,150, 114,50, 114,200
270 DATA 114,200, 114,200, 114,150, 114,50
280 DATA 101,100, 114,100, 127,100, 150,100
290 DATA 127,240
```

Pages 30-31

ROW, ROW, ROW YOUR BOAT:

(Lines 170 to 200 are given on page 30.)

```
210 DATA MER ,96,50, RI ,96,50, LY ,96,100
220 DATA MER ,127,50, RI ,127,50, LY ,127,100
230 DATA MER ,150,50, RI ,150,50, LY ,150,100
240 DATA MER ,192,50, RI ,192,50, LY ,192,100
250 DATA LIFE ,127,100, IS ,142,100, BUT ,150,100
260 DATA A ,170,100, DREAM ,192,255
```

JOLLY GOOD FELLOW:

(Lines 170 and 180 are given to you on page 31.)

```
190 DATA HE'S ,114,200, A ,114,100, JOL,114,100
200 DATA LY ,127,100, GOOD ,114,100, FEL,101,240
210 DATA LOW ,127,200, FOR ,114,100, HE'S ,101,200
220 DATA A ,101,100, JOL,101,100, LY ,114,100
230 DATA GOOD ,101,100, FEL,96,240, LOW ,75,200
240 DATA WHICH ,75,100, NO,85,100, BOD,75,100
250 DATA Y ,85,100, CAN ,96,200, DE,114,100, NY,127,240
```

Pages 32-33

SKIP TO MY LOU:

```
170 DATA LOST ,75,100, MY ,75,100, PART,96,100
180 DATA NER ,96,100, WHAT,75,50, 'LL ,75,50
190 DATA I ,75,100, DO? ,63,200
200 DATA LOST ,85,100, MY ,85,100, PART,101,100
210 DATA NER ,101,100, WHAT,85,50, 'LL ,85,50
220 DATA I ,85,100, DO? ,71,200
230 DATA LOST ,75,100, MY ,75,100, PART,96,100
240 DATA NER ,96,100, WHAT,75,50, 'LL ,75,50
250 DATA I ,75,100, DO? ,63,200
260 DATA SKIP ,85,100, TO ,85,50, MY ,71,50
270 DATA LOU ,75,100, MY ,85,100, DAR,96,200
280 DATA LING ,96,200
```

FRERE JACQUES:

```
170 DATA 127,100, 114,100, 101,100, 127,100
180 DATA 127,100, 114,100, 101,100, 127,100
190 DATA 101,100, 96,100, 85,200, 101,100
200 DATA 96,100, 85,200, 85,50, 75,50
210 DATA 85,50, 96,50, 101,100, 127,100
220 DATA 85,50, 75,50, 85,50, 96,50
230 DATA 101,100, 127,100, 127,100, 170,100
240 DATA 127,200, 127,100, 170,100, 127,200
```

Pages 32-33 (cont.)

TOM DOOLEY:

```
170 DATA 170,50,  170,100,  170,50,  150,100
180 DATA 127,100,  101,200,  101,200,  170,50
190 DATA 170,100,  170,50,  150,100,  127,100
200 DATA 114,200,  170,50,  170,100,  170,50
210 DATA 150,100,  127,100,  114,200,  114,200
220 DATA 114,50,  114,100,  101,50,  127,100
230 DATA 150,100,  127,200,  170,50,  170,150
240 DATA 150,100,  127,100,  101,200,  101,200
250 DATA 170,50,  170,100,  170,50,  150,100
260 DATA 127,100,  114,200,  170,50,  170,150
270 DATA 150,100,  127,100,  114,200,  114,200
280 DATA 114,50,  101,150,  127,100,  150,100
290 DATA 127,200
```

Pages 36-37

SHENANDOAH:

```
170 DATA 170,100,  127,100,  127,100,  127,200
180 DATA 114,100,  101,100,  96,100,  75,100
190 DATA 85,240,  63,100,  67,100,  75,255
200 DATA 85,100,  75,100,  85,100,  101,100
210 DATA 85,240,  85,200,  75,100,  75,100,  75,200
220 DATA 85,100,  101,100,  127,100,  114,100
230 DATA 127,240,  170,200,  127,255,  134,100
240 DATA 127,100,  101,100,  85,255,  127,100
250 DATA 114,100,  101,240,  127,100
260 DATA 114,200,  127,200
```

Page 39

MICHAEL ROW THE BOAT ASHORE:

```
170 DATA 142,100,  114,100,  96,150,  114,50
180 DATA 96,50,  85,150,  96,200,  114,100
190 DATA 96,100,  85,255,  96,200,  114,100
200 DATA 96,100,  96,150,  114,50,  107,50
210 DATA 114,150,  127,200,  142,100,  127,100
220 DATA 114,240,  127,100,  142,200
```

Page 40

quarter, half, quarter

eighth

whole

Page 42

MARIANNE:

(DATA lines 170 and 180 are done for you on page 42.)

```
190 DATA 85,200,  71,100,  71,100,  101,200,  85,200
200 DATA 85,100,  96,100,  75,200,  1,1,  75,100
210 DATA 75,100,  63,100,  63,100,  96,200,  75,100
220 DATA 75,100,  75,100,  85,100,  71,200,  1,1
230 DATA 85,200,  71,100,  71,100,  101,200,  85,200
240 DATA 85,100,  96,100,  96,200,  1,1
```

Pages 43-44

TELL ME WHY:

(Use with MUSIC WORDS.)

```
170 DATA TELL ,170,100,  "",150,100,  ME ,134,100
180 DATA WHY ,127,100,  "",101,150,  THE ,114,50
190 DATA STARS ,127,200,  DO ,150,100,  SHINE ,170,240
200 DATA TELL ,170,100,  "",150,100,  ME ,134,100
210 DATA WHY ,127,100,  "",101,150,  THE ,101,50
220 DATA I,114,100,  "",150,100,  VY ,101,100
230 DATA TWINES ,114,240,  TELL ,170,100,  "",150,100
240 DATA ME ,134,100,  WHY ,127,100,  "",101,150
250 DATA THE ,114,50,  O,127,200,  CEAN'S ,114,100
260 DATA BLUE ,101,240,  AND ,101,100,  I ,96,100
270 DATA WILL ,101,100,  TELL ,150,100,  YOU ,114,150
280 DATA JUST ,127,50,  WHY ,134,100,  I ,101,100
290 DATA LOVE ,114,100,  YOU.,127,240
```

HE'S GOT THE WHOLE WORLD IN HIS HANDS:

(Use with MUSIC RESTS with modifications from page 44.)

```
170 DATA HE'S ,114,50,  GOT ,114,50,  THE ,114,50
180 DATA WHOLE ,114,200,  WORLD ,134,50,  "",170,150
190 DATA "",8,8,  IN ,114,50,  HIS ,101,50
200 DATA HANDS ,114,100,  HE'S ,114,50,  GOT ,114,50
210 DATA THE ,114,50,  WHOLE ,127,200,  WORLD ,150,50
220 DATA "",181,150,  "",8,8,  IN ,114,50
230 DATA HIS ,101,50,  HANDS ,114,100,  HE'S ,114,50
240 DATA GOT ,114,50,  THE ,114,50,  WHOLE ,114,200
250 DATA WORLD ,134,50,  "",170,150,  "",8,8
260 DATA IN ,114,50,  HIS ,101,50,  HANDS ,114,100
270 DATA HE'S ,114,50,  GOT ,114,50,  THE ,114,50
280 DATA WHOLE ,114,100,  WORLD ,114,100
290 DATA IN ,127,50,  HIS ,150,150,  HANDS.,170,255
```

Music Symbols

LENGTHS OF NOTES

𝅝 Whole note	255	
𝅗𝅥 Half note	200	
𝅘𝅥 Quarter note	100	
𝅘𝅥𝅮 Eighth note	50	
𝅘𝅥𝅯 Sixteenth note	25	

𝅗𝅥. Dotted half	240
𝅘𝅥. Dotted quarter	150
𝅘𝅥𝅮. Dotted eighth	75
𝅘𝅥𝅯. Dotted sixteenth	37

NAMES OF NOTES AND THEIR VALUES:

NOTE	NATURAL	SHARP	FLAT
A	56	#52	♭59
G	63	#59	♭67
F	71	#67	
E	75		♭80
D	85	#80	♭90
C	96	#90	
B	101		♭107
A	114	#107	♭120
G	127	#120	♭134
F	142	#134	
E	150		♭160
D	170	#160	♭181
MIDDLE C	192	#181	
B	203		♭215
A	228	#215	♭241
G	255	#241	

OTHER MUSIC SYMBOLS

♯ Sharp   ♭ Flat

♮ Natural

▬ Whole Rest   ▬ Half Rest

𝄽 Quarter Rest   𝄾 Eighth Rest

𝄿 Sixteenth Rest

$3.95

Computer Fun Series
from
ENRICH/OHAUS®
THE GOOD IDEA PEOPLE

The **Computer Fun Series** will provide you with a variety of exciting and easy to use programs and procedures. Almost every page includes an instant reward either on your screen or on your printer.

Suggestions for you to try appear throughout the series. All are great incentives to see what you can do with your computer. You'll soon be changing the programs or procedures and then moving on to create your own.

The **Computer Fun Series** is not only fun to use, but is an excellent learning experience.

APPLE FUN is a collection of games and activities to help learn BASIC programming. General knowledge of computers is gained through a varied selection of word puzzles. Programming fun is accomplished with clocks and timers, coins and dice, and number guessing games.

APPLE MUSIC turns your computer into a musical instrument. You will learn to read and write your own music to play or include in other programs. Play and sing along with *Worried Man Blues, Tom Dooley, Freres Jacques* and much, much more.

APPLE GRAPHICS is an introduction to low-resolution graphics. It starts with simple graphing activities and progresses through animation. Uses of random colors are also explored. Switch a flashlight on and off, see a fish swim in a tank and witness an erupting volcano.

APPLE LOGO is designed as an introduction to Turtle graphics. Programs are written in Apple Logo, but conversions to MIT Logo (Terrapin and Krell) are included. The turtle is directed to draw many fascinating and creative shapes and designs. Color can be used to heighten their visual appeal.

More titles are coming soon. Write for your free **ENRICH/OHAUS** computer catalog.

*Ask for the **Computer Fun Series***
wherever good books are sold!

0   30531 79253

Printed in the U.S.A.
ISBN 0-86582-167-4